Where beauty has no ebb, decay no flood,
But joy is wisdom, Time an endless song.
—William Butler Yeats

A Time to Keep

The TASHA TUDOR Book of Holidays

Written and Illustrated
by TASHA TUDOR

Rand McNally & Company
Chicago   New York   San Francisco

Library of Congress Cataloging in Publication Data
Tudor, Tasha.
A time to keep.

SUMMARY: Describes traditional holiday celebrations
throughout the year in a New England household.
1. Holidays—New England—Juvenile literature.
(1. Holidays—New England)   I. Title.
GT4805.T83   394.2'6974   77-9067
ISBN 0-528-82019-2
ISBN 0-528-80213-5 lib. bdg.

Time is the image of eternity.

— Plato

To every thing there is a season,
and a time to every purpose under the heaven:
...a time to keep.

—Ecclesiastes

Granny, what was it like
when Mummy was like me?

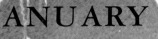

JANUARY

January brings the snow,
Makes our feet and fingers glow.
—Mother Goose

Oh, there were lots of joyful times.
On the last day of the old year the children built a bonfire.
We all danced around it and shouted Happy New Year.

Then we had a party supper

with roast beef and Yorkshire pudding

and apple pie and ice cream and cheese.

January sixth—that's Twelfth Night—
the children took out the four goat sleighs and had races.
It was great fun.

There was a prize for the winner.

In the evening everyone dressed up
and played charades.

FEBRUARY

Roses are red, violets are blue,
Angels in heaven know I love you.

—Old Song

We had a small post office in those days.
Valentines came by Sparrow Post.

The doll family received valentines.

So did all the corgis.

And Miss Puss got a catnip mouse.

On Washington's Birthday we had Washington pie for tea

and favors sent from Boston by Aunt Middle Mary.

In the evening the children put on historic tableaux
using the costumes we still have in the attic.

MARCH

Daffodils, that . . . take
the winds of March with beauty.
—William Shakespeare

March brought sugaring weather

and everyone turned out to gather sap.

Syrup making ended with a sugaring-off party

when we ate dinner at the sugarhouse
and had sugar on snow for a treat.

APRIL

April showers
Bring May flowers.
—Mother Goose

Easter week we all made pretty Easter eggs

and had hot cross buns for tea.

We always had the most wonderful Easter egg tree
with goose, duck, chicken, bantam, and pigeon eggs.
On the very top were canary eggs.

In April the new kids were let out to play
in the warm spring sunshine.

There were calves to feed

and little chicks.

And there were always gaggles of goslings.

MAY

Welcome be thou,
faire, fresshe May.
—Geoffrey Chaucer

On May Day the children left May baskets
at our neighbors' doors.

And we danced around a Maypole.

That's the month we planted the garden.

We had delectable elevenish parties
with iced tea and cookies
under the crab apple tree.

JUNE

And it was summer—
warm, beautiful summer.
—Hans Christian Andersen

Midsummer's Eve comes in June.
That's when we had a marionette show.
There were many, many rehearsals—

marionettes to make—

scenery to paint—

and programs to print and color.

The play was at night in the carriage shed.
Grandmothers had the very best balcony seats.

Refreshments were served at the intermissions
and everyone had a wonderful time.

JULY

Life, Liberty
and the pursuit of Happiness.

—Thomas Jefferson

July Fourth started with setting off firecrackers under tin cans.
The boys loved the noise. But the corgis didn't!

We would hang the flag from the loft window

and fix a huge and delicious picnic.

Then we would take the canoes
and paddle to the magic island
where we ate lunch.

In the evening there were fireworks
at the fairgrounds in the village.
We liked to watch them from the high pasture.

AUGUST

My heart is like a singing bird.
—Christina Rossetti

August brought your mother's birthday
which we celebrated at night by the river.
The table was set with birch bark plates and gourd drinking cups.

There were favors made from walnut shells

and families of wooden animals in little baskets

and meringues made in the shape of toadstools.

But best of all—

the birthday cake came floating down the river.

SEPTEMBER

Comfort me with apples.
—Song of Solomon

September is fair month.
On Labor Day we used to hold the Dolls' Fair.

All the dolls came, of course,

and their friends.

We used buttons for money.
You could buy cakes and pies and anything else you wanted—
all for buttons.

It was great fun.

There was a flower and vegetable show with prizes—

beetle races—

archery contests—

and delicious ice-cream sodas.

OCTOBER

When the frost is on the punkin
and the fodder's in the shock.
—James Whitcomb Riley

October was the time to make cider

and pumpkin moonshines.

And what exciting Halloween parties we had!

NOVEMBER

No fruits, no flowers, no leaves, no birds,
November!

—Thomas Hood

On Thanksgiving we roasted the turkey before the fire.

So many relatives came to visit
that the children had to sleep in the barn.

We did plays and charades
and had a literary contest
with a handsome book for first prize.

That's the month we made Christmas presents

and a year's supply of candles.

DECEMBER

Some say that ever 'gainst that season comes
Wherein our Saviour's birth is celebrated,
The bird of dawning singeth all night long.

—William Shakespeare

Christmas was the best of all times to keep.
On December sixth, St. Nicholas's birthday,
we put up the Advent calendar and the Christmas pyramid.

We lighted the Advent wreath
and had a St. Nicholas cake for tea.

Christmas Eve was a magical time.
When dark fell we stepped into the starlit night
to follow a winding path lighted by candles

to an enchanting crèche in the woods.

And on Christmas night
we had the loveliest celebration of the year

with the beautiful tree in a shine of candles
to remind us of peace on earth and loving kindness.

And that's how it was when your mother was a little girl.

TASHA TUDOR

And that's how it still is. Holiday traditions rooted in Tasha Tudor's own childhood were recreated, with embellishments, for her own four children. Now they are renewed for her grandchildren. The Sparrow Post Office is still in use for valentines. Advent calendars appear each December 6. Marionettes are refurbished and newly costumed for plays. Melissa, the special love of the artist's childhood, reappears at dolls' fairs.

Tasha Tudor, one of America's most loved illustrators, was born in Boston and grew up in Connecticut, the daughter of a portrait painter and a designer of yachts. She has lived her entire life in New England, for many years in New Hampshire and at present in Vermont. Her first book, *Pumpkin Moonshine*, appeared in 1938. There have been more than 40 books since that time.

A Time To Keep brings together all the qualities for which Tasha Tudor is famed. The delicacy of her watercolors. The nostalgic and imaginative settings. The intricate borders with which she prefers to surround her illustrations. Avid gardeners will recognize flowers, grasses, and herbs of New England. Friends and acquaintances will recognize her home, her corgis, her family and friends.

For all who would know more of Tasha Tudor, she is a spinner, a weaver, a seamstress, an admirer of the art of Eastman Johnson and Winslow Homer, a cook, an omnivorous reader, a "passionate" gardener. Above all, she is a painter who is able to translate her joy in a flower, her happiness in a task performed well, her pleasure in the turning of seasons, her appreciation of traditional values, into a form that speaks eloquently to readers everywhere.

DATE DUE

APR 28 '83		
FEB 25		
FEB 25 '86		
MAR 2 4 1990		
MAY 2 4 1990		
GAYLORD		PRINTED IN U.S.A